D1325382

Series Editor: Simon Melhuish
Editor: Heather Dickson
Authors: Simon Melhuish & Jenny Lynch
Page design and layout: Gary Sherwood and Gary Inwood Studios
Cover design: Gary Sherwood

Death on the Dockside, Death in Chinatown & One Deceased Dame were
written by Jenny Lynch.
All other puzzle stories by Simon Melhuish.

Published by:
LAGOON BOOKS
PO BOX 311, KT2 5QW, UK

ISBN: 1899712453

SIXTY SECOND
MURDER
PUZZLES

YOU ARE THE DETECTIVE!

Other titles available from Lagoon Books:

FANTASTIC OPTICAL ILLUSIONS & PUZZLES (ISBN 1899712402)

WHERE IN THE WORLD AM I? - MYSTERY GEOGRAPHY PUZZLES (ISBN 1899712410)

AFTER DINNER GAMES (ISBN 1899712429)

TRULY AMAZING MIND-BOGGLERS! (ISBN 1899712445)

PUB TRIVIA QUIZ (ISBN 189971250X)

MIND-BENDING PUZZLE BOOKS

MIND-BENDING LATERAL THINKING PUZZLES

(ISBN 1899712062)

MORE MIND-BENDING LATERAL THINKING PUZZLES - Vol. II

(ISBN 1899712194)

MIND-BENDING CONUNDRUMS & PUZZLES (ISBN 1899712038)

MIND-BENDING CLASSIC LOGIC PUZZLES (ISBN 1899712186)

MIND-BENDING CLASSIC WORD PUZZLES (ISBN 1899712054)

MIND-BENDING CROSSWORD PUZZLES (ISBN 1899712399)

MYSTERY PUZZLE BOOKS

DEATH AFTER DINNER (ISBN 1899712461)

MURDER ON THE RIVIERA EXPRESS (ISBN 189971247X)

MURDER IN MANHATTAN (ISBN 1899712488)

DEATH IN THE FAMILY (ISBN 1899712496)

50 OF THE FINEST DRINKING GAMES (ISBN 1899712178)

LATERAL DRINKING PUZZLES (ISBN 1899712208)

TRIVIA ON TAP - BAR ROOM BANALITY (ISBN 1899712216)

LAUGHS ON DRAUGHT - PUB JOKE BOOK (ISBN 1899712224)

Books can be ordered from bookshops by quoting the above ISBN number.
Some titles may not be available in all countries.
All titles are available in the UK.

INTRODUCTION

This book contains a pocketful of crimes for you to solve. You are a detective who gets to shadow Harry Schultz, a New York homicide cop, as he goes about his work.

Schultz is fed up with life and tired of death, but he is still a top detective. By following him you pick up all the clues, meet the witnesses, hear all the evidence, and know everything that he knows.

By the end of each story, Schultz has solved the crime - and you have just 60 seconds to do the same.

Remember - a minute is a long time in the seedy world of crime!

(The answer to each murder puzzle is in mirror writing immediately after each story - this will stop an accidental glance spoiling the fun. Just hold the page up to a mirror for the answer to be revealed!)

INDEX

INTERNAL AFFAIRS

INTERNAL AFFAIRS

New York's a dirty city, and murder's a dirty crime - but someone's got to deal with it and most of the time that someone is me.

My name is Harry Schultz, and I work for the city police department. When there's a homicide in Manhattan they dial my number. A lot of the time the people who get wasted in Manhattan have it coming to them big-time. But no matter how low the low-life is that winds up in the morgue, I have to figure out who stiffed them. That's my job.

It was late - after midnight - and the rain was coming down like there was no tomorrow when I got the call. By the time I reached the scene I was wetter than a trout in the Hudson River, and about as cheerful. Krapovitz had beaten me there, which just made me madder - he knew this was a job for us, and not the Feds, but he just couldn't help sticking his goddamn nose into other people's business. In this case, mine.

"What are you doing here Krapovitz," I shouted, so's to be heard above the torrential rain; "ambulance chasing?"

"Just doing your job for you Schultz," he replied. "I was in the area."

"Was that before or after you heard the call on the radio?" I asked, but it went straight over Krapovitz's stupid head.

"Suicide, third floor" he told me, though I don't remember asking. "Shot himself in the head - not pretty."

I pulled myself up the stairs, my clothes dragging me down they were so wet. The building was cheap - mostly rented apartments, I guessed. The shabby stairwell was covered in spray paint graffiti - looked like they hadn't seen a paintbrush in about 30 years, though it was hard to see just how bad things were, what with the 15 watt lights that the cheap landlord had put everywhere.

There were eight bulbs in the hallway, two on the stairs going up, and another six on the first landing, though one was dead. I kept on walking, trying not to touch the walls with my shoulders, or put my hand on the stair-rail. I see some gruesome sights in my line of work, but I hate nothing more than dirt.

Panting heavily I reached the third floor. I didn't like to admit it but maybe the boys were right. Maybe I did need to lose a few pounds. Thinking of food, my stomach rumbled. It had been at least four hours since I had grabbed the last chilli dog - hell, a cop just has to grab what he can, when he can. He never knows when he's next going to get the chance to eat.

Forcing all thoughts of food to the back of my mind, I pushed the door open and entered the apartment. I didn't have to ask which one it was; Krapovitz already had some goons there, *my* goons as it turned out, from the station.

"Hey!" I shouted. "How come you guys turn out so fast when Krapovitz calls?"

"A neighbour reported a gunshot - they called 911. Krapovitz was already coming down the stairs when we got here," Schultz told me. He knew I liked Krapovitz just about as much as I liked dieting and going to the gym.

The apartment was number 314 and was brighter than the stairwell, and cleaner too. The corpse was male, 50 - 55 years and Caucasian. Around 5'11", I guessed. He was smartly dressed in grey flannels and a check sports jacket with black shoes. That was all I could see, he was face down on the floor.

The room looked like it had been used as an office. It had a desk, a nice one too, files, book-cases and that kind of stuff. The stiff had a revolver in his right hand, and the right hand side of his head - the side I could see - was a mess. The blood had run down his face and was staining the grey carpet in a crimson arc. The chair was pushed well back from the desk, at an angle.

"Any note?" I asked Schultz. He shook his head. "Keep looking - there'll be one somewhere." There always was. I must have seen a hundred suicides, and there was always some kind of note.

I stood between the body and the desk, where in my thinking he would have sat, because I guessed he would have written a last farewell from there. I don't know why but I pressed the PLAY button on an old Dictaphone that lay on top of the desk. I'd seen the model before; I used to have one just like it. We found the good-bye we were looking for straight away:
"I just can't stand it - I can't go on any longer" I heard a frightened voice say, followed by a single shot and the sound of someone slumping to the floor.

I studied the desk. There was a blotter in the centre of the desk, but I couldn't make out any indentations from anything he'd written resting on it. He'd been a tidy man, though, everything was neatly laid out - papers in a tray top right, telephone to the right of the blotter, the old Dictaphone machine below it, paper clips and bands in a little pot next to that, old fashioned ink pen and ink pot just to the left of the blotter, and a telephone note pad, with a pencil still in the holder, just to the left of that.

Nothing looked like it had been disturbed or knocked about, no reason to suspect a struggle of any sort had taken place here.

There are times when I wish I'd been a banker, or a gambler, or a shoe-shine boy - anything other than a cop - this was one of them. I studied the lights in the room, two lamps on the desk, both on, and a central rose hanging from the ceiling, turned off. I flicked the switch on the wall momentarily, on and off again, and the light flickered.

"Dust the whole place, top to bottom for prints," I told Schultz. "It's homicide."
"Oh, and pull Krapovitz's prints from the records," I added as an after-thought.

Why does Schultz suspect Krapovitz?
That's not so difficult, but how is he so sure it was murder and not suicide?

SOLUTION

He suspected Krapovitz because he'd been at the scene of the crime (and was coming down the stairs) before the officers from the station responding to the neighbour's call. How did he get there so fast?

Schultz further suspected foul play when he noticed that the pens, and most importantly the telephone note pad and pencil were to the left of the blotter. The victim was obviously left handed - a right handed man would have found it virtually impossible to use the note pad, particularly since the 'phone was on his right hand side - yet the gun was in his right hand, probably placed there by the murderer.

Most importantly though, when he pressed the play button on the Dictaphone, he immediately heard the message and the fatal shot. So who rewound the tape? If it had been a suicide, the tape would have started from the end of the message, not the beginning.

DIRTY WORK

DIRTY WORK

My first ever case, and my least favourite arrest, was to do with two brothers, the Delgardos.

Tony Delgardo I'd grown up with. I knew him well. We'd been like brothers until we reached fifteen. We'd gone to the same school, shared the same dates, fought each other's battles and told our Mamas and Papas the same lies.

Then Tony'd gone running off with some questionable gangs, and we'd parted company. But we kept in touch - Tony sometimes trimmed his sails a bit close to the wind, but he just about managed to stay on the right side of the law.

Then there was his brother Frank.....

Frank I had never met. Their mother had died when they were both small, and they had gone to live with two different aunts. Tony with his Aunt Luisa in the Bronx and Frank with his Aunt Cissy in San Fran. Though I'd never had the pleasure of meeting Frank face-to-face, never even seen a picture of him come to think of it, I knew of his reputation. Frank's reputation was big. In fact Frank's reputation was huge.

Where Tony had managed to toe the line, Frank had jumped over the edge. He'd started out as a small time crook but over the years, things had gotten worse. He was never going to reform. It was a vicious circle. They put him in prison, he served his time, he came out and robbed some store so they put him in prison again. When he got out again, guess what? He robbed a bank, and so it went on.

There was a rumour that kept going round that Frank was 'connected' - but in my experience the Mob had little trouble telling the difference between a sharp operator and a klutz like Frank.

All the same I was sorry the day that the call came from San Francisco saying that a woman had been found dead and that Frank Delgardo was the one with the smoking gun. He was believed to be heading back to New York, probably to get help from his family - that's why they called me.

No-one in the station realised I knew his brother, and I kept it that way. I don't take my personal life to work with me; it just gets in the way. In the kind of business I'm in, you don't need added complications. The way things had been for the past two years I didn't have a lot of personal life to get in the way anyhow, but that's a whole other story.

So I got into the car and went looking for the wretched Frank. Somehow I knew this wasn't going to be difficult. I grew up with a lot of kids who, sure as night is night, were heading for a life of small-time crime. I knew how they worked, how they thought.

As far as I knew, Tony hadn't met up with his brother in years but he was my first port of call.
    "Hey, Harry - long time no see."
    "Five years - my wedding," I reminded him.
    "Hey, yeh - how's.....". He hesitated. He was trying to remember my wife's, my ex-wife's, name. It was Tania, but I just shook my head. He said he was sorry.

I told him why I was calling, and from the look on his face, I could tell that he didn't know a thing. "Frank?" he said, and crumpled back into his easy chair, shaking his head back and forth muttering "No, no. Not little Frankie".

The grey-haired, old-timer sitting in front of me sobbing his heart out was not the Tony I remembered. He was a shadow of his former self and walked with a stick now, after being hit by a truck as he drunkenly tried to find his way back home one night.

In his prime, Tony had worked for the Gianni Rimini, one of the richest property developers in Manhattan. Tony had been his right hand man, his muscle, his fixer. I never liked to ask about the things he'd done for Rimini in those days. The professional side of me was happier not knowing.

When old man Rimini died - was murdered - Tony had worked for a while for his young widow, but she was killed less than a year after her old man. From there on, Tony's life had gone into slow motion free-fall. It made me want to cry.

I left him in his apartment and cruised round the streets low down on the East Side. I guessed that Frank would hit here before long, trawling the bars until he came across someone he knew, someone who could get him a job, fix him up with somewhere to stay. Tony had told me that there was no family left except himself, so the 'Frisco cops had been wrong about that. He also said that he was about the last person on earth Frank would turn to if he was in the kind of trouble I said he was.

There was no sign of him in any of the bars I checked and I'd been into quite a few. I even stopped off at Jimmy's Bar to see if Jimmy himself knew anything, but he was his usual genial dumb self, and professed to knowing no-one, hearing nothing, and seeing even less.

I was just about to give up on my hunch and head back to the station, when I saw a man get out of a car, and walk across a dirty bit of land that some kids were playing ball on. Something about the way he walked, or maybe his build, made me look.

"Hey mister!" one of the kids shouted; "throw us the ball!". A long kick had caused the ball to shoot away from them and past the man. As he turned to throw the ball back I saw his face.

I jumped out of the car, sprinted across the grass and flattened poor Frank before he had a chance to so much as mutter. He was so shocked he didn't even try to resist. I cuffed his arms behind his back and dragged him to his feet.

"Mister; you a cop?" one of the kids yelled. They'd all crowded round to watch the action and were standing staring, open-mouthed.
"Another day protecting and serving" I told them, and marched Frank across to the car.

Schultz's first arrest in New York was also his least favourite. But since he had never met Frank Delgordo, or seen so much as a picture of him, how did he manage to arrest the right man without even checking his name?

17

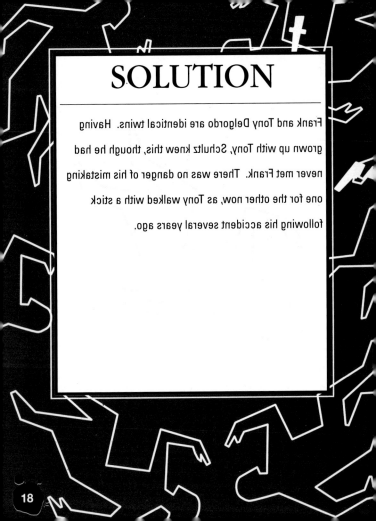

SOLUTION

Frank and Tony Delgordo are identical twins. Having grown up with Tony, Schultz knew this, though he had never met Frank. There was no danger of his mistaking one for the other now, as Tony walked with a stick following his accident several years ago.

18

AN ENGLISHMAN EXPIRES

AN ENGLISHMAN EXPIRES

I waved down a cab and as the driver weaved his way through the crawling traffic, I cursed my luck for being called out on such a foul night. The wind was howling like a hungry hyena and more importantly, I'd been drinking in Jimmy's Bar on East 44th, and I was not pleased at the interruption.

Jimmy's place has little to recommend it - it's dark, dull and smoky, and Jimmy himself is to bar tending what Fidel Castro is to ballet - but it's quiet and predictable, and after a day in Gotham city peaceful predictability is what I need.

But the call had come in from Pinsker, a good patrol cop. Unlike most of his kind, Bud had a big enough brain to figure out when I needed a call and when I didn't. He hadn't been wrong before, so I guessed he wasn't wrong now. So I'd finished my beer, said goodbye to the sultry blonde I had been schmoosing with, and made my way to Park Avenue, home of the rich, the famous, and tonight, the dead.

Pinsker stood on the sidewalk, looking worried, as the cab pulled up. I gave the cabbie a $5 bill, he grunted. I stayed put but he didn't offer any change. Too tired to argue, I got out.

As I crossed the road, a car screeched by splashing my newly pressed flannels. Cursing loudly I raised my fist and shook it at the black Cadillac speeding off into the distance. I reckoned the car must've been travelling at 60 miles an hour but I still managed to catch a glimpse of the driver.

I had only seen a flash of his face in the rear view mirror but there was no mistaking that sneer. It belonged to Tommy LaGarda, one of New York's Mafiosi and one of the States most wanted men.

As I wandered over to where Pinsker was standing, I wondered what a sleazeball like LaGarda was doing in this part of town.

"Shooting, first floor," Pinsker said without preamble, bringing me back to the case in hand. "Jeffrey Jones, a Limey. No Mrs. Jones recorded at this address."

"Big deal," I barked, my opinion of Pinsker taking a nose-dive. "So a non-resident living alone gets wasted and you call me on my night off?"

"It's not just any non-resident sir," he told me. "It's *the* Jeffrey Jones."

I'd heard about Jeffrey Jones, or at least I'd read about him. He was one of the richest 500 men in America, a hot shot property developer in Manhattan. And as Pinsker had already figured, you don't get to be a hot shot anything in New York City unless you know some pretty heavy hitters in the city, or you've slept with the Mayor. If I hadn't been so pissed at being called out and dirtying my clean pair of pants, I would have noticed it just from the house - you don't get to own a house like this on Park Avenue unless you've got more dollar bills than the Pentagon has phone lines.

Pinsker told me that the Limey had been shot. An old lady from next door at 9931 had heard the gun-fire, while out walking her Pekinese. She called the police at about the same time as someone from Jones's house - he wasn't sure who.

The woman, a 73-year-old divorcee going by the name of the Countess Margarithe Luella de Mar, had heard the shot around 9 o'clock. It was Summer, and according to the little lady, some of her neighbour's windows had been open when she walked past and she'd heard Jones shout
   "Arthur - what on earth are you doing?".

She said she knew it was Jones because of his accent, and heard the shot immediately after that, but didn't see anyone run out of the house.

A patrol car had been passing at the time - for once cops were in the right place at the right time. They heard the shot and pulled up, though the old lady appeared not to notice. They went straight in through the unlocked front door and found three of Jones's staff in the house.

"They're in there waiting for you," Pinsker said. "His driver, his bodyguard, and his butler believe it or not. The patrol are fairly sure that no-one had time to get out of the house before they arrived."

I braced myself for the sickening sight of yet another corpse, and climbed the three or four steps into the house. Inside it was beautifully cool, a welcome respite from the unrelenting heat of an August afternoon in the Big Apple.

The floors of the mansion were tiled with white marble and the walls covered in enormous great paintings. I'm no Picasso but even I could see they were worth a buck or two. Shaking my head in disbelief at how the other half live, I walked into a room that stood immediately to the left of the entrance hall, over-looking the street.

Jones lay crumpled on the floor, his head towards the window, face exposed, legs half hidden beneath a writing desk. It looked kinda like he had been standing behind the desk when he was shot, the force of the bullet knocking him backwards as he fell.

His face registered only shock, not pain - I removed his spectacles and closed the eyelids. He had been hit in the chest, a large red stain was soaking through his English tweed waistcoat, around the point of the bullet's entry.

The gun lay on the floor close to the body; a small, easily concealed, German-made pistol of a type I'd not seen before. I smelt the weapon through force of habit - it had been fired recently. On the other side of the body lay a plain white cloth, the sort used to polish wine glasses, and another pair of spectacles (not the ones he had been wearing) with one broken lens.

The curtains were not drawn and one of the windows was slightly open, allowing a refreshing breeze and some of the sounds of the avenue to echo round the room. Running an expert eye around the room I took in a comfortable-looking three-seater sofa and two deeply upholstered reading chairs, arranged around a huge, handsome fireplace with a grey-green marble surround.

A small coffee table stood behind the sofa. Although I lay no great claims to knowing anything about interior decorating it seemed oddly placed to me, marooned in an otherwise empty space.

I saw from the indentations in the carpet that it had previously rested two feet further into the room, away from the windows, and had only recently been moved, though I couldn't figure out why that should be so.

There were very few ornaments on display; just a few writing implements on the desk, a globe on the coffee table, and a matching pair of pewter vases on the mantelpiece, of which only one contained flowers. Between them stood an ornamental china dog, a Pekinese, of such horrible design that I wondered what it was doing in this otherwise elegant room.

In the bin, I found a crumpled sheet of paper. I reached down to pick up what turned out to be a letter, written by the deceased.

The content simply baffled me further....

Count Leopold Luella de Mar

9931 Park Avenue

August 28

Having exchanged contracts on the above mentioned property (9931 Park Avenue) with the owner Max McGinty, you and your wife have 30 days from today to vacate the property.

I wish to thank you in advance for your co-operation.

Jeffrey Jones

Jeffrey Jones

Jones Conglomerates Inc.

I put the letter into my pocket and turned to face the Englishman's staff, who Pinsker had rounded up and brought into the study.

The driver was sitting in the armchair nearest to the window. You could tell by the full chauffeur's uniform, including driving gloves and cap. The butler, easily recognised by his manner if nothing else, was standing stiffly by the fireside, as if awaiting further instructions from his master. He'd been brought over from England by Jones, as if you needed telling. The third of the group, the bodyguard I assumed, sat at the far end of the sofa, looking frightened and shocked.

I've seen a lot of guilty people in my time, and a few innocent ones too, and if nothing else, I know that there's no way to tell the difference just by looking at them. But in this case it was different.

I didn't feel like playing Hercule Poirot, making everyone listen to my theories, so I just walked up to the butler, took him by the arm and led him out to the car.

Schultz had indeed arrested the murderer, but how had he been so certain about who to arrest without needing to ask any questions? What had he seen which implicated the butler?

SOLUTION

It was easy. He was fairly sure that 'Arthur' had fired the shot (as the old lady had reported), and he knew who 'Arthur' was since both Jones's driver and his bodyguard were female.

RUNNING SCARED

RUNNING SCARED

It was a sunny Sunday morning so I'd pulled up at Central Park. I'd decided to take in some of the smoggy city air to try and get rid of the fog that lingered in my head, courtesy of too much drink the night before. And the night before that, and the one before that too.

They say an alcoholic is someone who drinks more than their doctor - I've never met a doctor who could drink as much as me, so I guess I have got a problem.

Never straying far from the car, I was trying hard not to get mowed down by the crazy rollerbladers, the mad cyclists, and the endless stream of marching activists. Central Park on a Sunday is more dangerous than Fifth Avenue on any day of the week - at least the taxi drivers on Fifth have some kind of control over their vehicles. I'd just started thinking about my daughter, when the car radio crackled - it always seemed to happen that way.

It was Dorkins at the station. They had a suspect in for interview, and although it wasn't a homicide case, there was something about the set up that made Dorkins think that maybe I should get involved. That at least was something of a surprise - not the homicide, but the news that Dorkins was thinking.

He was assigned to assist me, to ride with me, and I didn't

have a lot of choice in the matter. He was a nice enough guy, but asking Dorkins to solve a crime is like asking a three-year-old to explain the finer points of quantum physics. My theory is that Dorkins has the right number of brain cells, it's just that they're not connected up in any way. But he's pleasant enough to have around, and he's good with a gun, so I could've done worse.

By the time I got down to the precinct the weather had turned nasty - big black clouds rolled in from New Jersey, and some fat blobs of rain started hitting the windscreen just as I pulled up to the kerb and parked illegally. One of the perks of being a cop in New York - you can park in no - waiting zones. Big deal. After the twenty yard sprint from the car to the front entrance of the station, I was as wet as one of the stiffs we sometimes pull from the East River. The rain had gone through my coat, my jacket and my shirt - I could feel them sticking to my shoulders.

The guy was in the interview room. I stood looking at him through the blind. He was about thirty five, weedy-looking, smoking a cigarette and biting his fingernails.

He looked nervous, but no more jittery than you or I would be if we'd been dragged in by the homicide squad. The only people in this place who didn't look nervous were the hookers they dragged in downstairs, and that was just because they'd all been here so many times before. To some of them the precinct was as good as a second home. While I was watching him, Dorkins gave me the details.

His name was Dick Arnold and he was a high school teacher. He'd called 911 at 7.30 this morning, having woken up to find his wife dead in the bed beside him.

"Or so he says," said Dorkins with heavy irony.

The wife was older than him, 52, a teacher at the same school. She had something of a weight problem, Dorkins told me with a smirk. It seemed that the paramedics had some difficulty getting the body out of the house.

The beat cops who'd turned up at Arnold's door didn't find anything to suggest foul play, but something had made them twitchy about the case, so, not wanting to be suspected of going soft or anything, they cuffed him, dragged him down to the station, and handed him over to us. All this to a man whose wife had just died in her sleep.

"What the hell is he doing here?" I asked no-one in particular, and went into the room.

I gave him my condolences and apologised to him for the over-eager behaviour of the boys in blue. I explained that since he was here I was going to have to make a report, so he was going to have to tell me what had happened, but if we made it short and snappy I'd release him and have one of the patrol cars take him home.

"We went to bed at about eleven," he began. "Me and Patricia both read for a while - Pat's been having trouble sleeping lately, so she likes to read as long as she can. She was reading one of those horror books, and I kept telling her she shouldn't - it wasn't good for her. And then it happened - she had the nightmare again. She's been having a lot of nightmares recently, though they're all different, they absolutely terrify her.

"She wasn't in the best of health you know, she hardly ate anything, but she weighed quite a lot and couldn't seem to lose weight. The doctor had told her, I think, that she was looking to have a heart attack if she didn't exercise some, but she didn't anyway. I think she had a great fear of exercise, or maybe just a fear of ridicule. I think she could see herself jogging down the sidewalk, and all the neighbourhood kids were jeering and laughing at her.

"So, like I said, she had this nightmare - this time she was running down the freeway, faster and faster, and one of those huge trucks was bearing down behind her." He took another cigarette from the packet and lit it.

"At first when she looked back she could see the whole truck. Then she could only see the metal grill, then just the fender, and it got closer and closer until finally, it slammed into her back and everything went black. Then I guess her heart gave out, what with the shock and all, and... and..." He stopped and wiped his eyes.

I looked away to give the poor man a bit of privacy. While looking round the room, my eyes caught a number on the back of the match box, which Arnold had been using. I scribbled the number down, passed it to Dorkins and asked him to run a check on it.

"I'd been telling her for months now," Arnold continued, "that she really should listen to the doctors, and get fit or something. I'd been expecting something like this to happen for a long time - I can't pretend it's a surprise, but it's still such a shock.

"You know, we were out in Central Park a couple of weeks ago, and we had just walked from the lake across to Madison Avenue - you know, it's not like it's a huge distance - and Pat had to sit on one of the benches for half hour to get her breath back. I should have known then. I should have put her in the car and taken her straight to the hospital. I don't know how I'll ever forgive myself."

He stopped talking for a while and stared at the wall. I excused myself, and left the interview room in search of Dorkins.

I found him in the refreshment canteen, tucking into a round of jam and apple doughnuts. He looked like a cat that had caught a mouse and eaten all the cream.

"Got it boss," he said, "number belongs to a certain lady of the night who's all too familiar with the comforts of a police cell. Goes by the name of Saucy Sue - real name Susan Delaney - she's been busted maybe five times in the past six months. Said she'd been seeing Arnold on and off for the best part of a year."

I picked up one of the doughnuts and sunk my teeth into it. After chewing for several seconds, I'd made up my mind.

I told Dorkins that we'd be holding Arnold a while longer, that I wanted to talk to the woman's doctor, and that I wanted an autopsy done on the body. I had a horrible feeling that Dorkins was right and I'd been wrong - we had another murder on our hands.

Why had Schultz changed his mind?
Surely being unfaithful did not necessarily mean he was a murderer?

SOLUTION

Schultz's suspicions had been raised when the husband went to great lengths to stress how unfit his wife was, and how she had been expected to have a heart attack. But when Arnold told him about his wife's fatal nightmare he knew he was lying, for he said that she died suddenly - of a heart attack - and that he'd found her dead in the morning. In which case, there is no way he could have known what she had been dreaming about.

DEATH IN CHINATOWN

DEATH IN CHINATOWN

My hand hit the receiver before the second ring had
sounded. No matter how long I've been asleep, the sound
of a telephone always has me as wide awake as an alleycat
in a fish shop.

My two hours sleep had been fitful anyhow. New York's
degenerates and psychopaths were beginning to haunt my
dreams. Hell, even a 3am phone call's better than that.

"Schultz?"
"Yeah?"
"Homicide...Chinatown." The words landed like lead in my
belly. I needed a tussle with the triads like I needed a hole
in the head. Like I needed a broad like Delilah. Bits of last
night came into my mind. Delilah may be one hell of a
dame but the dame was becoming demanding and it was
more than I could handle right now. Anyhow, no time for
that now.

It was 3am and a homicide needed fixing. I reached for my
cigarettes. It was going to be a long day.

The lights of the cop cars made the murder scene easy to
find. What do you know...it was the very street Delilah and
I had strolled down only hours before.

Before the big bust up; before the tears and screaming had
started.

Someone filled me in on the details:
   "Someone called the station...don't know who...unable to
trace the call....no witnesses...time of death 'bout an hour
ago...." The words were becoming all too familiar.

I went straight to the victim. He was depressingly young -
early twenties I'd guess. He was one cool dresser too -
alpaca coat, shiny new brogues and grey tweed suit and
waistcoat.

One shoe-lace was untied and his left cuff-link was missing.
There was a small tear in his shirt, just above the left cuff.
There was dirt under his fingernails, looked like fresh earth.

The stiff had had his throat cut. Expertly. The fine line right
round his neck was not like anything I had seen before.
Or maybe once before.

I called to mind the handiwork of one Spikey Muldoon.
Him and me had stalked each other round the streets of
Brooklyn the Summer before.

If I hadn't known for certain that Spikey was safe behind
bars now, I'd have sworn....... Then I thought that things
were bad when you find yourself standing admiring a

murderer's handiwork. Maybe Delilah was right. Maybe it was time to move upstate.

Wallace appeared. He was the new kid at the station. I realised from his flushed face that this was his first homicide. That and the fact that he was shaking uncontrollably. Better get used to it kid.

   "Anything found with the body?" I asked.
   "Yes sir. A gun and a briefcase full of new dollar bills - a protection racket I guess."
   "Careful, kid. Nobody likes a smartass. OK, OK, go search the area."

I started to look through the victim's pockets.
   "Already done that sir."
Christ. At least this time he had the decency to look humble about it.

It seems we'd got a wallet containing a photograph of one very classy lady - looked a bit like Delilah - one lighter and a piece of paper with something scribbled on it.

The pencil marks were faint, but if I held it up to the light I could just make it out.

3377719

"Looks like a telephone number sir."
Bright kid Wallace. Should go far.

I went to the car and put a call through to the station to get them to try the number for me. Things were definitely looking up. Maybe I'd be able to get some sleep before going down the station. Heh, maybe I'd even give Delilah a call tonight.

"Sorry Schultz," came the reply, "no such number in use. At least not in the New York area."

So all I had to go on was a telephone number which could be for anywhere. The wind started to howl down the street like a lone wolf.

I went back to the body which was about to be hauled off to the morgue. It was lying right across the sidewalk, in the shadow between two streetlights.

On one side of the street was a line of restaurants. Their shop signs were all the same; the name of the joint in red lettering with the name of the proprietor in smaller letters underneath: 'The Wong Wei' owned by W. Lee, 'The Lucky Fortune Cookie' owned by T. Cheung and 'The Dim Sum Temple' owned by H. Chait. Between each was an alleyway.

On the other side of the street was a Chinese supermarket, 'The Won Ton Shop' and an old movie house, long since boarded up. In between these was a stretch of waste ground. The sidewalk was littered with fortune cookie wrappers and garbage. What a place to end up. It started to rain, large puddles forming where the body had been.

Wallace and the guys had searched the area and spoken to the neighbours. Or at least tried to. Seems nobody speaks English round here. Or nobody's willing to. I looked around - no sign of a struggle anywhere.

   "Nobody knows the victim, nobody seen nothing, nobody heard nothing. Absolute zilch." Even Wallace was looking down in the mouth.

As I tried to light a cigarette the wind whipped the goddamn thing right out of my mouth and onto the ground. As I bent down to pick it up, the blood rushed to my head and suddenly everything fell into place.

   "OK guys. Search the Wong Wei again and this time I'm going in to ask a few questions. I'm sure we'll find our killer before too long. And Wallace, you come with me. You might learn a thing or two."

Since the telephone number was invalid, how did Schultz arrive at this amazing conclusion?

SOLUTION

As Schultz bent down to pick up his cigarette, he looked up at The Wong Wei and saw the proprietor's name W. Lee upside down. That's when he realised that he had been looking at the piece of paper upside down too. It wasn't a telephone number but the name Bill Lee - probably the Mr W. Lee on the sign.

THE PENTHOUSE
KILLER

THE PENTHOUSE KILLER

The last weekend in January is always the longest and coldest in my personal calendar. I'd spent most of this one losing myself in bottles of whisky at Jimmy's Bar. Then all of a sudden it was Friday, three in the morning, the darkest hour of the soul according to F. Scott Fitzgerald. By four o'clock I'd found myself again, and wished I hadn't.

It was too early to go to work, and too late to start on another bottle, so I just sat at the bar, reminiscing. The place was empty except for me and Hank. He had been a professional basketball player when he was younger - a lot younger - one of the best. I still remember seeing him play at Madison Square Gardens when I was no more than eighteen years old. Time and time again he would grab the ball, spin round the defence, drive to the basket and dunk the ball over the heads of the opposition. Brilliant player, a real pro.

Sadly, his career lasted as long as a trip on the Titanic; a bad knee injury put him out of the league too long for him to make a comeback. So now the former Knicks guard spends his days, and his nights, in Jimmy's, getting drunk.

I was thinking about this because I'd worked on a case the week before involving a basketball player. Jarvis was his name, and he played for the Knicks too - but it was thirty years since Hank had last played, so there was no point in asking him if he knew Jarvis. Hank didn't even watch the games on the TV anymore, so far as I knew.

A woman had been killed in Jarvis's apartment on the 50th floor of a block down on the Upper West Side. It wasn't that swanky, but it wasn't too run down either - it was one of those apartment buildings where the caretaker lives on the ground floor and keeps everything in good order. Jarvis had the best apartment in the building - a penthouse suite that occupied at least half of the top floor. Views over the city were amazing, but I had no time for that.

The girl was one of Jarvis's girlfriends, and she'd been found dead in the bathroom by Jarvis when he'd come home one morning. That was where she was when I found her, on the bathroom floor, lying in a pool of her own blood. She had been knifed in the chest. From the amount of blood on the floor I guessed the knife must've hit an artery, or maybe the heart. Pretty gruesome - it didn't look like a suicide.

The forensic boys were all over the place when I arrived. Maybe they got a tip-off. Maybe they were less hung-over than me when the call came in, I don't know. But when I'd finished looking at the girl they told me that she'd probably died at about five, five-thirty, just four hours earlier, and that, as I'd guessed, they figured from the angle of the wound that she was murdered.

"That runt Mulhearn killed her," Jarvis volunteered. I was just about to ask him what he meant when he told me he'd been out of the apartment since eight the previous evening with another woman, whose name and address I took down. He said he hadn't returned until 5.30am. As he came out of the elevator he said he had seen his neighbour, 'the little guy', walk out of this, Jarvis's apartment, and coolly walk back into his own, which was just across the hall.

Jarvis must have measured 6'11" in his socks, so I wasn't exactly sure what a 'little guy' was, until I went to interview Mulhearn. He was the smallest man I ever did see - couldn't have measured much over four feet max.

His story was that he too had come back around 5.30am, after his night-shift.

"You go straight to your apartment?" I asked, "or did you go visiting?"

"At 5.30 in the morning? Are you mad? I took the cage to the thirtieth floor and then walked up the last twenty, like I always do. But I didn't go visiting," he said. "And I certainly didn't go visiting *that* apartment." He nodded in the direction of Jarvis's door.

"Why d'you walk up the last twenty floors?" I asked him.

"I like the exercise, what do you think?" he said.

That was when I decided to get in the elevator and go down to talk to the caretaker. I asked him if he'd happened to be awake around four.

"Sure I was up," he said. "Sure I saw people around."

Do caretakers never sleep? I didn't like to ask. He said he'd seen two people come into the building. Not only that but he'd written down when they came in.

"You what?" It turned out he keeps a log of all the people who come in or out of the building. A tenants' nightmare but a detective's dream, I thought. Sure enough Jarvis had returned at 5.32 exactly, the caretaker said. Mulhearn had returned at 5.29, "just like always, give a minute or two".

Things were looking decidedly gloomy for Mulhearn. Jarvis's story seemed to hold up - Mulhearn had taken the elevator to the top floor and killed the girl, during which time the elevator had had time to go back to the first floor and bring Jarvis back up in time to see Mulhearn leaving the apartment.

It all made sense, except one thing. I got back into the elevator and on the way up, decided to pull my handcuffs from my belt. I was worried what would happen if a 6'11" basketball giant refused to come quietly.

Once again Schultz cracks the case. But why, in the face of two conflicting stories, has he chosen to believe Mulhearn and not Jarvis?

SOLUTION

Schultz is correct - Mulhearn was telling the truth and Jarvis was lying. They both entered the building at 5.29am and 5.32am respectively, as they said.

As Schultz realised, on the way back up to the 50th floor apartment, Mulhearn did go up in the elevator, but at only four feet tall he could only reach the button for the 25th floor or so, maybe the 30th at a stretch. There was no way he could have reached the button for the 50th floor. Jarvis, having seen him come into the building, figured that the timings were perfect for setting him up. What he failed to realise was, as Mulhearn had had to walk up twenty floors, there was no way he could have got to Jarvis's apartment before Jarvis himself. The girl could have been killed by somebody else in the building, but why would Jarvis lie about Mulhearn if he (Jarvis) was innocent?

50

MURDER AT THE WALDORF

MURDER AT THE WALDORF

The last thing I needed was a complicated homicide. I had been up since the crack of dawn wading through the police files down in the central precinct trying to do some background research on a guy name of Bugsy Capone.

Everyone knew he was guilty as sin but he was one slippery son of a bitch and it was always the same with him: when the evidence pointed his way, he was nowhere to be found and when he dared rear his ugly head above ground, there was nothing to stick on him.

I read through the files I'd requested but drew a blank. There was nothing. Zippo. Zilch. I guessed there was no other way but to get out onto the street. He was out there somewhere and I was damned if I wasn't going to find him.

So to cut a long story short, I'd walked round all day. I started at Pier 92, walked across town to Grand Central then south to Little Italy, where I grabbed a dog and a beer before heading into China Town.

Twelve hours and many more beers later, I'd spoken to most of my snitches and no-one was saying nothing. Word on the street was he was in town but where no one knew. Or if they knew, they certainly weren't saying.

I returned to my car and was heading home when I passed the precinct and noticed the light was on in my office. As there was no one at home keeping my dinner warm for me, I went in to investigate.

In spite of the light, the place was deserted. I grabbed a cup of black coffee from the machine and sat down at my desk. On top of the piles of paperwork, I came across a note and beneath it, a crime report I hadn't seen before.

The note from my sidekick Dorkins - "One for you to look at, Boss," it said. I glanced down at the scene of crime report. A shooting had taken place in the lobby of the Waldorf Astoria of all places.

Appetite whetted, I flicked on my desk light and settled down to read the rest of the report.

Three couples had been arrested at the scene - a fancy dress shindig in the Waldorf Ballroom. All six of the revellers knew each other and they all knew who the killer was, but because they knew we couldn't identify the murderer, they were all keeping stum. I couldn't believe it. This was the second wall of silence I'd come across in one day.

What the report did tell me was that one woman was wearing a black dress, another a white dress and the other a brown one. The men too were in black, white and brown, but it was clear that the couples were not paired by colours.

Witness reports, as usual, were a mess. More than 400 people had attended the ball, yet not one of them could be sure which of the men - they had noticed it was a man at least - had pulled the trigger. I read the whole report and scribbled notes as I went along. It was nearly two hours later by the time I finished.

Not much to go on. No wonder Dorkins, who was no rocket scientist, was confused. I stood up to stretch my tired legs and wandered across to the window. Outside it was dark and all was quiet, everyone had gone home to their wives and their children except me. Me and the sleazy villains of the world, who never seemed to need any sleep.

I walked back to my desk and re-read my notes.

- None of suspects would say who fired the gun.

- None of suspects would name their partners.

- One witness was sure that the murderer was the partner of the woman in black - she was certainly cracking up under the strain - BUT she wouldn't say which man was her partner.

- None of the couples were wearing the same colour.

-Six people had confirmed that the man in black was not the partner of the woman in white.

I re-read the last sentence I had written and felt my mouth break into the smug smile of a contented man. At last I had it.

With so little evidence to hand, how was Schultz able to identify the murderer when Dorkins before him had failed?

SOLUTION

Schultz was able to identify the murderer because the man in black must have been with the woman in brown - she couldn't have been in black because then they would have matched and she couldn't have been in white because the witnesses confirmed this.

Likewise, the woman in white couldn't be with either the man in white or the man in black - she must have been with the man in brown.

Lastly, the woman in black must have been with the man in white, and he, therefore, was the murderer.

ONE DECEASED DAME

ONE DECEASED DAME

I was heading for Jimmy's after a long day at the station when I felt a tap on my shoulder. Penhaligan had rings under his eyes and the haunted look of someone with a problem.

"I hate to ask you Schultz, but I'd sure appreciate some help on this one."

It looked like a clear-cut case to me but I liked Penhaligan. The guy had what I'd call integrity. He looked you in the eye. Besides I owed him one. Ever since that time he'd taken Cut-throat Kilroy out with a shot clean through the stomach. I reckoned listening to Penhaligan's problems was the least I could do.

"Let's go get a drink - you look like you could do with a large one."

Down at Jimmy's, hot jazz and hot broads swirled round like an arctic roll. But they'd have to wait. I tried to concentrate on Pen H's story.

Seems that some broad had been found dead right in the middle of Brooklyn Bridge. She'd been shot cleanly through the temple at close range. There was no sign of a murder weapon. No sign of a struggle. Looked every inch like a professional job, probably hired by someone who knew her. So far, so good.

Then things get kinda complicated.

The broad's lawyer contacted the station with a letter she had sent him six months earlier. It was an amendment to her will and she had left instructions that it was not to be opened until after her death. Penhaligan showed me a copy of it:

SEE PAGE 60

The husband was tracked down in a penthouse on the Upper East Side enjoying the not inconsiderable pleasures of a dame called Dolores Divani and in possession of two one way tickets to Paradise, going by way of Honolulu.

"So what's the problem, Penhaligan?" I asked. "That guy's got so much evidence stacked against him he's buried alive."

Mr. J. Thornton

Attorney at Law

Cooke, Bayke & Boyle

8635, 2nd Avenue

NY. NY.

If I should die in anything other than natural circumstances, I want the police to know that I'm certain my husband is plotting to kill me. He killed a man last year and I think he knows I know. I'm certain that he plans to kill me in order to protect himself. I want to leave but I'm too sacred - because then I'll know he knows I know.

Yours

J. D. Range

Doris D. Range.

"It just don't feel right Schultz. That guy must be one hell of an actor. I mean, either give the guy an Oscar or his wife's death really has knocked him sideways. He's making out she was unstable - you know - an English broad, feeling homesick, kinda depressed all the time."

"And Dolores Divani?"

"One dumb broad: I don't think she knows what time of day it is. And another thing, try as I might, I can't pin any other murder on this guy - though he's no Snow White that's for sure."

I left Penhaligan at the bar. This whole thing was a mess. I knew the whirling dames would swirl his way and I reckoned he could do with a night off. Me? I had other things on my mind. I decided to pay a late night visit to the deceased dame's home.

I knew it would be empty. It was a smart apartment in a run down part of town. The caretaker seemed all too familiar with late night cop visits and showed me to the third floor without uttering a word. The front door had seven different locks on it. Just what were they trying to keep out? Or in?

Inside everything was scrubbed and polished like a shoe-shine boy had worked overtime. Looked like happy families to me. But then I never was an expert on that kinda thing. The remains of a pot roast was in the refrigerator and an unbaked pecan pie sat on top of the stove.

It didn't look like anyone was planning to leave. Separate bedrooms though. His closets were full of good quality clothing. A bottle of expensive cologne stood on a dresser. Next to it was a pile of newspapers, a silk handkerchief and a penknife.

Her room was full of chintzy fabrics and little china dolls. There were piles of books everywhere: copies of Shakespeare sonnets and big fat novels. This lady had liked to read. That was something that I used to be fond of too when I was at school. I settled down in an armchair and reached for the nearest hardback. It was a collection of Sherlock Holmes stories. My favourite. I turned on the nearest lamp and started to read. Maybe Sherlock would inspire me now.

First thing next morning I was on the bridge. The air was not yet clogged with exhaust fumes and there was a strange peacefulness about the place.

The body had been found on the south-facing sidewalk. That was three days ago so there would be very little evidence around now. Still, like all good detectives I found myself checking the area. Besides I was looking for something specific. And I found it.

The bridge railings had been newly painted but I found a small circle, about half an inch across, where the paint had been knocked out and the metal exposed. The metal had not yet corroded so I knew that it was fairly new.

Once back at the station I found Penhaligan and suggested that he get divers to drag the river.

"Looks like a suicide to me," I added, "you should be able to release the husband soon. Oh, I nearly forgot - you'll be looking for a gun and some rope."

Sure enough within two days Penhaligan had the look of a much younger man.

"You were right Schultz - I've got the weapon and the rope. How come you figured that one out?"

How did Shultz figure it out? And more importantly, how did the woman kill herself?

SOLUTION

Schultz did get inspiration from one of the Sherlock Holmes stories - as had the wife. She must have realised that her husband was having an affair and her revenge was to stage her own murder in the hope that he'd spend the rest of his days in some stinking hell-hole of a prison. She had tied a rope to a gun and weighted it with a stone over the edge of the bridge. When she shot herself the stone dragged the gun over the edge and into the water, chipping the paintwork on its way.

CHRISTMAS CALL-OUT

CHRISTMAS CALL-OUT

When whoever it was made up that saying about no rest for the wicked, they forgot about us cops, for if there's no rest for the wicked, then there sure as hell's no rest for us.

In December, when the snow is thick on the streets - deep enough to stop the traffic running in places - and the Christmas lights are up and there are trees in the windows of just about every Fifth Avenue store, then everyone's thoughts should be turning towards a joyous Christmas and happy New Year. You would expect murders in the Big Apple to drop off a little. But no. There's always some scumball out there who can manage to take time off from their Christmas shopping to chill someone out.

Last year I got call at 23:55hrs on Christmas Eve - just five minutes before Christmas Day for Chrissake. It was a downtown robbery gone wrong and they wanted me to go down take a look.

My wife Tania was still living with me then. The look on her face when she realised I was going to be working through Christmas should have warned me that things were not going well, even then.

The NYPD boys had apprehended a man at the scene of the crime. A princely $500,000 had been taken from a man in a bar, in a mugging that had gone wrong and ended up as a murder. It seemed like the uniformed guys might have bungled it too though; the guy they'd arrested was a cab driver and he claimed to be an innocent bystander.

By the time I got to the station he was already in the interview room.

"He's deaf," Dorkins told me, "wouldn't talk to us without a sign-language translator present, so I called up for one."

"You found one on Christmas morning?" I asked in disbelief and he told me that she was on her way.

While we waited, I asked Dorkins where the killing had taken place. It was a bar I knew well, not socially mind because it was out of my neighbourhood and also because the Honky Tonk was a kinda loud, brash sort of place. Full of pin-ball machines, video games and that sort of thing. We'd searched the place a couple of weeks back after receiving a tip-off that it was fronting a gambling racket - something I'd suspected for years - but we couldn't find anything that'd stick.

After a good half an hour, the translator arrived. As she walked up the corridor towards us, I cast my expert eye up and down her body and sized her up in an instant. I noticed Dorkins do the same but she was no beauty. She had long skinny legs, a sickly-looking smile and no figure to speak of. Her name was Mabel.

I drew her to one side and asked her to do me a favour, then we both went into the room. The man was sitting at a table, with his back to the door. He didn't hear us come in - not surprising really. I drew up two chairs and Mabel and I sat down opposite him.

When I introduced myself Mabel started with her hands. The man watched her closely after each question, and then answered himself. His speech was good and clear for a deaf man - I guessed he'd not been deaf all his life.

He admitted he'd been in the bar where the robbery took place at 11.00pm but said that he'd been watching television near the back of the room, and - being deaf - hadn't heard a thing. He didn't even know anything had happened until it was all over.

He answered all my questions reasonably and sensibly. Once or twice the translator nodded at me. He stuck to his story, and there were no flaws in it so far as I could see. He was just an innocent guy having a drink who was in the wrong place at the wrong time. All the patrol cops had on him was that he was leaving the bar as they arrived. A witness leaving the scene of a crime? Hardly a high court felony.

But all the same, it just didn't stack up.

  "Ask him what time he arrived at the bar again," I told the translator. Again he said 8.00 o'clock.

"You talk to anyone?" I asked.

"Not all evening," he replied.

"What were you drinking?"

"Coke," he said.

"What was on the TV?"

"The Mets game, and before you ask, the Mets were winning."

I got up and went out to find Dorkins. In the hallway the festivities were hotting up, Kurtz and O'Hara were wearing red Santa Claus hats and someone had turned the radio on. Jingle Bells was just starting up.

"Lock him up until the 27th", I said. "I'm going home."

"What do I charge him with Boss?" Dorkins asked.

"Accessory to murder," I told him, and went home to try and enjoy what was left of Christmas.

Why did Schultz not believe the man's story?

SOLUTION

Schultz's suspicions were raised because the man said he was a cab driver. If he was deaf, how did he know where his fares wanted to go to? To test his theory, Schultz took the sign-language translator to one side and asked her to mis-translate some of his questions. Since the cab driver managed to answer the questions which Schultz asked, rather than the ones the girl signed, Schultz knew that he was not deaf at all. And if was lying about that, he was obviously trying to cover something up.

THE WASHINGTON
WEEKEND

THE WASHINGTON WEEKEND

Sometimes I feel like I'm jinxed. When you get a call in the middle of the night telling you there's been another murder in the neighbourhood, and your head's fuzzier than a grizzly's arse on account of the week's wages you blew in Jimmy's Bar the night before, you kinda wonder whether you're responding to the homicides or they're just happening because you're there. You get to thinking that maybe if you went back to bed it'd all go away.

I felt that way in Washington - I was there on account of a conference that had been called for all the hot shot detectives from across the good ol' US of A.

Why my name was on the list I'll never know but as to why Washington was the host town I can certainly guess.
If you're going to host a homicide convention where better than in a city where the chances of you getting blown away by some sixteen-year-old punk with a shotgun are about the same as you getting a parking ticket in any other city in the world.

Being away from New York, I figured I was getting away from work - at least from the dirty end of the job - for two whole days, but I figured wrong. By my second day, there I was up to my neck in the dirt and grime of an investigation all of my own.

How I got to be appointed out of all those hundreds of homicide cops that were there was simple - I witnessed the murder. Or rather, I almost witnessed it.

See, I was drinking in a bar called 'Norms' for a lot of the first evening. It was a Friday and I'd met up with an old buddy who was working out of Houston, and we'd decided to have a drink or two for old times sake.

We'd ended up in a bar not that far from our hotel. We had a table by the bar, drank a few beers, caught up on the past eight years or so and left around twelve. Midnight seemed a bit early to me but Chuck had wanted an early night. He insisted he needed a good night's sleep what with the jet lag and the fact that we were expected to turn up at the convention hall at nine the following morning.

We'd just walked out when we heard the shots, two in a row. 'Oh Christ' I thought, and walked back into the bar, where the gunfire had come from.

The corpse was lying flat on the floor. It looked like he'd been sitting at the bar on a stool, and had been shot in the back. Since no-one had left by the front door except us, it seemed a fair guess that the killer was still in the room.

I looked around. I hadn't noticed before, but there were just four other guys in there - probably the meanest looking bunch of men you could have gathered together in one place, even in Washington, and that's saying something.

I waited for the squad to arrive and had them all carted off to the station.

I missed the rest of the convention. I spent the next two days questioning the gang of four.

They all knew who had done it of course, but they weren't inclined to share the information with yours truly. What's more, they weren't easy to intimidate. They'd all of them had more close shaves than you could find in a barber-shop, so I wasn't going to scare them with threats of accessory-to-murder charges.

They might have been mean, but they weren't that smart - or at least not as smart as they thought they were. After two days, they'd given me a few things to go on, but not enough to nail the murderer, or so I thought until I re-read my notes.

They were called Tom, Max, Roman and Tristan Fellini - not brothers, but cousins from one big happy Italian family.

From questioning them, I'd figured out that at midnight that Friday, one was reading the paper, one was drinking at the bar and another was asleep, head on his arms on a table in the corner. The other must have been the one who shot the customer.

I'd also learned that Tom wasn't the one who was asleep, and he was illiterate, so he wasn't reading the newspaper.

Max doesn't drink, and was also illiterate.

Tristan wasn't asleep, and keeping to family tradition, couldn't read.

Roman wasn't sleeping, and wasn't drinking either.

Somehow I'd also gleaned the information from Max that if Roman was not the one who shot the customer, then Tom was not drinking.

At last, I'd broken it. They thought they had been so smart, the slimeballs, but from what they'd told me I'd figured out which of them was the killer.

So who was it? And how did Schultz know?

SOLUTION

It had to be Tom.

Roman was reading the newspaper, Tristan was drinking and Max was sleeping.

If Tom was not drinking then Tristan had to be.

Tom is the only one who was not drinking, reading or sleeping, so he was the killer.

A BROADWAY
FINALE

A BROADWAY FINALE

I was dreaming of a far-away land where the sun always shines and where there's an endless supply of cold beer and hot broads, when the phone rang, rudely returning me to reality.

"Shooting on the corner of Second Avenue and 31st Street boss, we'll meet you over there," shouted Dorkins.

It was 9.35 on a cold Sunday morning and Saturday night had been a long one. I dragged my tired body out of bed and took of a swig from the mug at my bedside. Bad move - it was whisky. I swallowed the mouthful, grabbed my pistol, scooped up my badge and my car keys and was on the road within five minutes, images of ice cold bud and wanton women long forgotten.

It had snowed during the night and it looked like the snow-plough drivers had suddenly discovered religion, they were so late getting going. By the time I got to the house, my Chevy had spent more time moving sideways than it had going forwards, but somehow I managed to get there without causing anyone or anything any serious damage.

A man had been shot the night before, but the body had only just been discovered by the housekeeper, an elderly woman by the name of Mrs Parker who'd dialled 911.

When I arrived at the scene of the crime, Dorkins was already there. He filled me in.

The stiff's name was Jack Wainwright. I knew the name immediately. Most of New York knew him as a load-mouthed, opinionated, loathsome Broadway producer. Nobody liked him it seemed, but he knew how to get the paying punters onto the seats, and in show business, that's what counts.

There'd be no shortage of suspects in this case, I thought - half the Big Bagel would've been more than happy to send the movie mogul off to the big theatre in the sky.

It took a long time for anyone to answer the door and when it was, it was only opened a crack. An old lady's face appeared in the gap, you could see her keen blue eyes squinting through glasses with lenses that looked like bottle ends, only thicker.

"What do you want?" she barked in an approximation of New York friendliness. She opened the door a little further, in the hope of getting her face a little closer to mine I suspected, so that she could see who I was - she was pretty short-sighted.

When I'd explained our business she let us into the house; and what a house. It had been a standard New York four-storey house, if you can call something like that, in that location, standard. Wainwright had had the entire structure gutted, and replaced the levels with part-solid landings and floors made entirely of glass.

A huge metal staircase wound its way from just to the left of the door right on up to the fourth floor - you could see it all the way. I was about to comment on the architecture when the housekeeper let out an involuntary sob, reminding me why I was there.

She gestured for us to follow her up the staircase. The nails in my shoes rang eerily on the stair treads in the otherwise silent house.

"I found him when I came down to work this morning," she said, leading into a kind of room on the second floor.

Like the apartment, this was no ordinary room. It had two solid walls, a third made of glass, and where the fourth wall should have been, there was nothing at all - the side was completely open, apart from a rail, overlooking the well that ran from the top to the bottom of the building.

On the floor was Wainwright's body. It lay face down, with a small bullet wound in his back. I turned him over slightly with my foot, just enough to see an equally neat bullet wound in the chest. The bullet had passed right through the victim. Whether he had been shot from the front or back I couldn't tell.

"Where was he when he was shot?" I asked the housekeeper. I could see Dorkins thought this an odd question, but something about the way he was lying seemed unnatural - I thought maybe he had been moved or something. The old woman's eyes, which were strangely magnified by her spectacles, flicked upwards.

I walked up the metal staircase to the room immediately above. The main floor area didn't extend as far into the building on this level, and the fourth wall was, again, nothing more than a low rail overlooking the stairwell. I looked over the edge. Wainwright had been shot on this floor, and his body had fallen to the room below.

I looked around the apartment to see where the bullet had wound up. It wasn't difficult - there would have been more decoration in a Trappist monk's cell. The furniture was minimal, there wasn't an ornament in sight and every vertical surface was a sheet of white, completely devoid of all objects save one, a clock, which the bullet had hit.

It had passed straight through the deceased's body and shattered the glass on the huge black and white clock that hung on the wall over the stairwell. It must've struck something in the mechanism as the clock had stopped at exactly 11.54. I glanced at my watch, it was now 10.55 in the morning.

I led the housekeeper down to a room on the first floor, away from the body, and asked her if anyone had visited the previous evening.

"Only Cameron Fyfe. He came to dinner last night, just

him and Mr. Wainwright. I served them myself what with Saturday being the cook's night off."

"And no one else came into the house all evening?" I asked.

"Not that I saw."

"So what happened, did they argue, did they fight?"

"Not that I know of," she told me stiffly, "they were business partners and the best of friends."

Like husbands and wives, I knew business partners were seldom the best of friends, but I didn't say anything. Instead, I asked "When did Mr. Fyfe leave?"

"10.59 precisely."

"Precisely?" I repeated.

"I looked at the clock as I locked the door. I'd been waiting for him to leave, so I locked up, looked at the clock and went to bed."

"Which clock?" I asked.

"The big clock on the stairs," she replied. "It's the only clock in the house. Mr Wainwright would only have the one clock in the house. He could be so particular about things like that." She went on to say that Fyfe had left in a bit of a hurry, almost knocking her down as he left. No-one else had come into the house as far as she was aware.

I told Dorkins to check the house for signs of a forced entry. There were none - I knew there wouldn't be. And I guessed that the elderly housekeeper was hardly going to be a prime suspect in the case.

"Put out an APB for Cameron Fyfe. First degree murder." I told Dorkins.

"But Wainwright died at nearly midnight sir, and Fyfe left an hour earlier!" Dorkins complained.

"I know," I said pushing my hands deep into my pockets and heading towards the door, leaving the Sergeant to make the necessary calls.

Schultz was sure that Fyfe had killed Wainwright - but according to the housekeeper, he left almost an hour before the clock was stopped by the bullet and there was no sign of a forced entry, so how did he do it?

SOLUTION

Schultz had noticed from the start that the housekeeper was extremely short-sighted. When Fyfe ran from the house and she locked the door she looked at the clock and saw the time as 10.59. Schultz realised that this was too much of a coincidence, since at 10.59 the hands of the clock are in exactly the same position as at 11.54, but transposed. The housekeeper had seen the clock after the murder exactly as it was now, but had mis-read the time. With no other clocks in the house, she didn't realise her error. Fyfe had left the house at 11.54 - just after committing the murder.

DEATH ON THE DOCKSIDE

DEATH ON THE DOCKSIDE

The witness was jumpy, but I was feeling confident. This was the chance I'd been waiting a lifetime for. More than a chance I'd say: a dead cert of getting Snakey Snazz banged up for good.

Snakey was the meanest man on the streets. His real name was Joey Snazz but I called him Snakey on account of the trail of slime he usually left in his wake. That and his habit of sneaking free just when you were about to close in on him. I didn't like him but I had to respect him. The guy was a survivor. But all that was about to change.

The evidence was good. Our witness was one Huey Fermoy. Huey was what you would call a reformed character from the Lower East Side. Last Tuesday morning he just happened to be standing down on the docks, waiting for a business associate and minding his own business.

He could hear two guys arguing over on the next pier but his view was kinda obscured by a pile of packing crates. Being a naturally curious kind of guy, Huey walked down to the end of the pier that he was waiting on.

From there he could see the whole of the pier next to him clearly reflected in the water. Dirty that water may be but the light was good and our man Huey had a ringside seat.

He saw two men. One was about 5'6", with dark hair a beard and a Hispanic accent. The other was 6 feet tall, white haired and lean featured. He also had a limp. My skin tightened.

That's our man Snakey. Had to be. The shorter man had looked desperate, like he wanted to escape. At this point, he became hidden behind the tall man so that all Huey could see was the tall guy's back. But he clearly saw the tall man pull a gun out of his right hand pocket, raise it and fire it once.

He then ran off towards the dock, dragging his left foot slightly. The victim was one Fernandez Hermandez, a flunky to one of New York's major drug barons. The guy would not be missed and in some ways, Snakey had done us a service. But it was the last one he'd do for a while.

Huey had picked Snakey out in the line up. The case was nearly tied up and I was feeling good as we went into the final interview. Snakey had hired some hot shot lawyer from Detroit, would you believe it. The guy was as smooth as glass and just as sharp. He made my skin creep almost as much as Snakey did.

"OK. Let's get this over with. One last time Huey, tell us exactly what you saw." It went like a dream. Huey even drew us a picture. Van Gogh he aint, but it was exactly what I wanted to see.

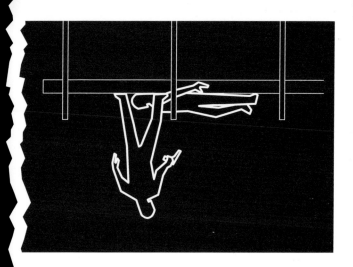

Asked for the third time in as many minutes, Huey said he was absolutely sure that this was the man he saw shoot the victim on the pier.

"In which case, gentlemen," lisped our Detroit dandy, "I take it you'll be releasing my client now?" Cool as a cucumber. "Your witness says that he saw my client pull a gun from the pocket on his right and fire. Correct?" Nothing wrong with Dandy's ears then.

"Need I remind you that this was a reflection, everything was reversed. So the killer, whoever he was, would have been using his left hand." My head started to hurt. He took Huey's picture and swivelled it 180 degrees, so that it was the right way up. It didn't take a genius to realise that the gun was actually in the man's left hand.

"My client is right handed. He couldn't fire a gun with his left hand if he tried." Goddamn it the creep was starting to smile. "You've got the wrong man. You've got to release my client."

I went out onto the plaza and lit a cigarette. Five minutes to collect my thoughts. I watched the people going past. All oblivious to the fact that some no good hoodlum was about to be let loose on them again. Could I really be wrong about this one? I stared down into the fountain water.

"Schultz? We got a case or what?" Dorkins' voice came from behind me.

"A case? You bet we got a case. Book him."

What the lawyer said makes sense, so what had Schultz noticed that made him discount the lawyer's argument and believe that Snakey really was guilty?

SOLUTION

The lawyer's reasoning is incorrect. If a mirror is if a mirror is parallel to an image it does reverse things from right to left, but when it is at 90 degrees to the image (as the water was in this case, more or less) it reverses top to bottom INSTEAD of right to left. Simply turning the drawing 180 degrees does not give the correct image. Huey realised when looking into the fountain that if he saw the gun drawn from the right side of the body then that WAS the man's right hand side.

DEMITRI'S DEMISE

DIMITRI'S DEMISE

There are days - and nights - when New York gets to feeling like the lousiest, meanest, dirtiest, foulest city in the world. Three in the morning, August 13th, was one of those times. The temperature was up in the high twenties, and I was sweating like a pig. So much so that I couldn't sleep.

I'd been thinking about my daughter, wondering what she looked like now. I missed watching her grow up and was feeling more miserable than those poor fools who jump off some of this city's many bridges, and take that long, dark, final swim in the river.

The phone rang. It was Dorkins.

"Suicide," he said, as I arrived at the apartment block on the Lower East Side. "Locked himself in his room and shot himself through the head." God, I hate suicides.

The man sat slumped in the armchair, a pistol on the floor at his side.

"Name's Dimitri," Dorkins continued. "That Russian or something?"
I shrugged. I didn't know.

The apartment was a sad, damp studio. It smelt like something else had died in there a long while before - something apart from the Russian that is. Small freezer, two ring stove, a tattered table with a single chair and TV, that was it. I opened the freezer, for no particular reason at all, and looked in. There was bottle of Vodka, some ice in an old plastic ice tray, and a loaf of bread that I wouldn't have fed to the ducks in Central Park.

On the shelf above the gas fire were three books - not exactly highbrow - and a couple of nasty looking statues of animals - dogs, I think they were meant to be. A huge picture hung on one of the walls - at least I think it was a picture. I guessed it was modern art but from where I stood, it looked as if the painter had been involved in a fight with a grizzly bear and it wasn't the painter that had won.

I went to the door - the only door into or out of the room - and looked at the lock. Despite the damage caused by the guys kicking their way into the room, it was still possible to see how it worked.

The door had been locked shut with an old fashioned drop-latch on the inside - the sort where a flat piece of metal simply drops down into a latch. There was no way to open or close the latch from the outside. It was impossible also to slam the door as you left and have the door latch behind you - someone had to be on the inside to lift it up to allow the door to close in the first place.

The latch served the single purpose of allowing someone inside the room to stop anyone else entering. There was only one tiny window, high in the wall, too small for even a child to crawl through.

I was just about to agree with the suicide theory and get off the scene when I noticed a small wet patch on the floorboards next to the door. I tasted it - water. I looked around the frame for a pipe that might have leaked - nothing.

"Any of you guys bring any water in here?" I asked the forensic team. They looked at me as if I was mad. What did I think they were, amateurs?

"Found a note sir," Dorkins cried and he handed me a sheet of paper torn from a notebook. (See Opposite) It was written in an unusually elegant hand, completely at odds with the sleazy surrounds.

I thought for a while and suddenly it all made sense.
"I think I'd better hang around here," I told the guys.
"It's another murder."

How does Schultz think that the murder was committed since the victim was alone in the room and the door, which could only be locked from inside, was locked when the police arrived on the scene?

To whoever finds me—

I cannot live with myself any longer,

therefore I must shoot myself. My

secrets are too terrible to ever reveal,

so I pray that they will die with me.

D. Popoff

SOLUTION

The killer shot Dimitri, forged a note and left it and the gun behind to make the murder look like a suicide. Before leaving the dead man's bed-sit, he had taken an ice-cube from the freezer and used it to prop up the latch on the door. He then closed the door carefully behind him. As the cube melted, the latch dropped, locking the door in his wake. The only tell-tale evidence was a small damp patch on the floor.